GRACE

What is It?
How Do You Grow in It?

Dirk Waren

Soaring Eagle Press

GRACE: What is It? How Do You Grow in It?

ISBN: 978-0-578-78138-9
PUBLISHED BY SOARING EAGLE PRESS
Youngstown

Printed in the United States of America

*God opposes the proud
but shows favor (grace) to the humble.
- James 4:6 & 1 Peter 5:5*

CONTENTS

give her his address and provide an accurate picture of where he lives. Or he could say, "flee from your house — just drive from your house as fast as possible and don't look back." Do you see the difference? In both cases the woman's going to leave her house. That's guaranteed.' 61

1

What is God's Grace?

You hear a lot about "grace" in Christian circles, but what is it exactly? In the Bible it's translated from the Greek word *charis (KAIR-iss)*, which means "graciousness, favor, kindness." Consider a "teacher's pet" in a positive sense. Why is a certain student the "teacher's pet"? Simple: That student has the teacher's favor. Now let's apply this to God's favor; that is, God's grace. Just as the teacher's pet has the teacher's favor so you and I can have *God's* favor.

But how do we obtain God's favor/grace? It's simple:

> **...Scripture says:**
> **"God opposes the proud**
> **but shows favor** *(charis)* **to the humble."**
> **James 4:6**

> **"God opposes the proud**
> **but shows favor** *(charis)* **to the humble."**
> **1 Peter 5:5**

Both James and Peter were quoting Proverbs 3:34 (albeit in koine Greek). So this phrase is shared **three times** in God's Word — once in the Old Testament and twice in the New Testament. Do ya think the LORD's trying to get something important across to us? Obviously: *Don't* be proud because God opposes — *resists* — the proud; rather cultivate **humility** because God gives his grace/favor to the humble. Simply put, **humility attracts the LORD.**

Now humility is *not* self-loathing. It's crucial to grasp this. Humility simply means you don't think you're all that and a bag of chips. Those with a humble spirit are *teachable*. It's a healthy, attractive quality and we'll look at why humility attracts God and his favor shortly.

In this book we're going to explore two forms of God's grace:

1. **God's grace (favor) of eternal salvation.** This, of course, includes all the benefits that come with salvation, like the forgiveness of sins (Ephesians 1:7), spiritual regeneration (Titus 3:5) and the apprehension of eternal life (John 3:36 & 1 John 5:11-12).
2. **God's grace (favor) for you personally, as you grow spiritually.** If you find this incredulous, Jesus Christ — our *example* — *grew* in God's grace (favor) when he was on Earth (Luke 2:52) and the epistles clearly exhort **us** to *grow* in God's favor (2 Peter 3:18 & James 4:8).

The trait of **humility** is going to be emphasized in this book because this is the quality that attracts God's favor/grace. Along with humility, we're going to examine two qualities that spring from humility — **repentance** and **faith**. We're also going to consider two types of love in the Bible, which relate very differently to God's grace.

The reason this book is important is because there's a lot of error about God's grace in the body of Christ today. This includes error concerning the linking topics, especially repentance. A top example would be the erroneous idea that God's grace is "unconditional." Really? If this were so, then *everyone* would have it. It's true that God's favor is unmerited in the sense that you cannot work for it or purchase it, but **there *are* conditions to receiving it... *and* growing in it**. If this weren't so, then *everyone* would have it — or *will* have it — and that's Universalism, a blatantly unbiblical doctrine.

I should stress that this work is rooted in **what God's Word teaches about grace** and not what this or that sect/camp/popular minister teaches. Thankfully, the Scriptures are simple and unmistakable on the topic.

Let's start with...

2

God's Grace (Favor) of Salvation

Notice how the awesome gift of eternal salvation is **linked to** God's grace:

> **In him <u>we have redemption</u> through his blood, the forgiveness of sins, in accordance with the riches of <u>God's grace</u>** *(charis)*,
>
> **Ephesians 1:7**

> **and all are <u>justified freely</u> <u>by his grace</u>** *(charis)* **through the redemption that came by Christ Jesus.**
>
> **Romans 3:24**

> **For <u>the grace</u>** *(charis)* <u>**of God**</u> **has appeared that offers <u>salvation</u> to all people.**
>
> **Titus 2:11**

> **For it is <u>by grace</u>** *(charis)* **you have been saved, through faith — and this is not from yourselves, it is the gift of God —** [9] **not by works, so that no one can boast.** [10] **For we are God's handiwork, created in Christ Jesus <u>to do good works</u>, which God prepared in advance for us to do.**
>
> **Ephesians 2:8-10**

Eternal redemption and all of its benefits are available to all people by God's grace. In other words, **God is extending the hand of favor — and the eternal salvation that goes with it — to all people** as a gift. A gift — as Ephesians 2:8-9 shows — is *not* something that comes from ourselves through performing religious works; it's a gift from a giver and you cannot work for it. In this sense God's grace of salvation is unmerited and this explains the definition of grace you'll often here from Christian ministers as "unmerited favor." But, technically speaking, the word 'grace' — *charis* in the Greek — doesn't mean "unmerited favor," it simply means "graciousness, favor, kindness."

While God's grace of salvation is an unmerited gift, the individual has to *receive* this gift; he/she has to *accept* it. In other words, although the gift of eternal salvation is unmerited and therefore you *cannot* work to get it or purchase it, this doesn't discount the fact that it needs to be received.

There are two things necessary in order for people to receive a gift:

1. They have to know there's a giver with a gift for them to receive.
2. They have to be willing to receive the gift, which is where humility comes into play.

Let's say a rich distant relative leaves you $1 million when she dies. It's in the bank for you to receive. But you can't receive it if **1.** you don't know about the giver and her generous gift and **2.** you don't go to the bank and get it.

Concerning the second one, I remember an occasion years ago when a family I knew was struggling financially. So I went to their apartment and handed the wife a $100 bill (which would be equal to about $250 today due to inflation), but she waved it off. She refused it. Why? I don't know. Perhaps she was too proud to take "handouts." I'm not sure, but she declined the offering. I walked away a little sad that she wouldn't receive my gift. This shows that, just because someone offers a generous gift, it doesn't automatically mean everyone will receive it.

It's the same with God's gracious gift of salvation and all that goes with it, like the forgiveness of sins and eternal life: Some people will choose to reject it. Why? Usually I suppose because they don't think it's legitimate; in other words they *don't* **believe**. Perhaps they stubbornly adhere to secular humanism or this or that religion/ideology, which they feel is good enough for them and more valid than John 3:16 & Romans 6:23. Another possible reason is pride. Maybe they think they don't need it for one reason or another, like they deem themselves good enough as is to merit God's favor and eternal life.

This brings us back to that attractive characteristic which is *requisite* to receiving God's grace/favor…

Humility, the Key (or Key Ring) to Receiving God's Grace

Let's go back to our fundamental verse — James 4:6 — but this time we'll look at the verses before and after as well, which is the context:

> Or do you think Scripture says without reason that he [God] jealously longs for the spirit he has caused to dwell in us? **6** But he gives us more grace *(charis)*. That is why Scripture says:
>
> "**God opposes the proud**
> But **shows favor** *(charis)* **to the humble**."
>
> **7** Submit yourselves, then, to God. Resist the devil, and he will flee from you. **8** **Come near to God and he will come near to you**. Wash your hands, you sinners, and purify your hearts, you double-minded. **9** Grieve, mourn and wail. Change your laughter to mourning and your joy to gloom. **10** **Humble yourselves before the Lord, and he will lift you up.**
>
> **James 4:6-10**

Verse 6 stresses that God shows graciousness **to the humble**. This is conveyed **three times** in the Bible, as pointed out in chapter **1**. It reveals a vital truth about God's favor and how to unlock it in your life. 'Humility' in the Greek is *tapeinophrosune (tap-i-nof-ros-OO-nay)*, which means "inner lowliness" or "lowliness of mind." It's not self-loathing or self-belittlement, but rather a healthy sense of one's littleness in the grand scheme of things regardless of position, possessions or talents. It's a modest opinion of oneself and describes a person who depends on the LORD first and foremost rather than self. A humble person is **pliable** and **teachable** whereas an arrogant person is obstinate and unteachable. You could explain humility as an inside-out virtue which is naturally produced when comparing oneself to the Almighty Creator rather than to other people, which of course helps keep one from being a self-exalting, self-inflated blowhard.

Have you ever met someone who regularly brags on himself or herself? It's a huge turn-off, isn't it? If it's a turn-off to you, how do you think the LORD feels about it? This explains the words of wisdom: "Let someone else praise you, and not your own mouth; an outsider, and not your own lips" (Proverbs 27:2). Write this on the tablet of your heart!

Two good examples of humility in the Bible are Moses (Numbers 12:3) and David (1 Samuel 18:23). It goes without saying that God used these men greatly, which is why over 3000 years after their passing people all over the world still talk about them and their exploits, like we are right here. They were mighty men — very talented individuals — but they were also genuinely humble, which is what attracted God's favor and explains why the LORD was able to use them so mightily.

The Creator's favor/graciousness/kindness is wonderful and God offers his grace to everyone, regardless of race, ethnicity or location. This indicates that God has **no favoritism**. But the LORD does not give favor to the proud who are too proud or too stubborn (one way or another) to recognize it, let alone receive it.

Now someone might point out that God "is kind to the ungrateful and wicked" (Luke 6:35) and "He causes his sun to rise on the evil and the good, and sends rain on the righteous and the unrighteous" (Matthew 5:45). This shows the LORD's **general grace toward**

fallen creation — God's kindness — which is intended to attract people to the Creator and the grace of salvation.

Unfortunately, many proud souls disregard God's general grace and scoff at the Almighty, even denying God's existence; some palpably hate the LORD or any notion of an Almighty Creator (Psalm 14:1 & 53:1). Why? Sometimes because they're disillusioned about God due to some tragedy; and their limited understanding holds them back. But often simply because they don't want any moral restraints in their life so that they can practice one pet sin or another.

God is greatly patient with such people (2 Peter 3:9) and we're called to pray for them (Matthew 5:44), but if they stubbornly continue in their arrogance, hatred and unbelief — disregarding God's general grace, not to mention any additional grace offered to them through the intercession of the saints — they're not going to receive God's grace of salvation. And, if they're too stubborn to recognize & receive the LORD's grace of salvation they're certainly not going to grow in personal grace, like Christ did (Luke 2:52) and Peter instructed us to do (2 Peter 3:18). Why not? Because — again — **God opposes the proud, but gives his grace to the humble!**

And this reveals…

3

The Two Keys to Receiving God's Grace of Salvation

While God's grace of salvation is unmerited — meaning you cannot work for it or buy it — it *still* has to be received in order to possess it. If this weren't so then *everyone* would be saved, which is Universalism, a false doctrine easily disproven in the Scriptures.[1]

There are two keys to receiving God's grace of salvation, **both of which spring from genuine humility** (as opposed to false humility). In light of this, you could say that humility is the **key ring** to God's grace, which holds two keys, the first one of which is…

---

[1] See the article on Universalism at the Fountain of Life site for details.

Faith

We observed last chapter how faith is key to receiving God's grace of salvation in this famous passage:

> **For it is <u>by grace</u>** *(charis)* **you have been saved, <u>through faith</u> — and this is not from yourselves, it is the gift of God —** [9] **not by works, so that no one can boast.**
>
> **Ephesians 2:8-9**

God's grace of salvation is received **through faith**. Why? Christ implied the answer in these two statements: "I tell you the truth, anyone who will not receive the kingdom of God like a little child will never enter it" (Mark 10:14) and "the kingdom of God belongs to such as these [children]" (Matthew 19:14). The Lord wasn't encouraging childish behavior, of course, but rather childlike trust — *faith* — and all that goes with it: humility, innocence, receptivity and lack of self-sufficiency in regard to the Creator and the Lord's kingdom. This is meekness or humility. It draws God's grace, whereas arrogance repels it.

Faith is vital due to the fact that:

> **...<u>without faith it is impossible to please God</u>, because anyone who comes to him must believe that he exists and that <u>he rewards those who earnestly seek him</u>.**
>
> **Hebrews 11:6**

Without faith it's impossible to please God. Reflect on that; it's an axiom.

What exactly is faith? Faith is belief, but not in the sense of believing in fairy tales; nor is it casual mental assent. Faith is simply **belief based on God's revelation**. Now, understand, God reveals truth — reality (including the Reality of his existence) — through various sources in addition to the written Word of God, although God's Word is where we learn *specific* spiritual truths and develop genuine doctrine. For instance, the Creator reveals himself through everything that he has created (Romans 1:19-20). So faith is *belief* based on **1.** what is intrinsically obvious, **2.** accurate knowledge, whether scientific, spiritual or otherwise, **3.** genuine revelation by the Holy Spirit, or **4.** some combination of these three.

Let's consider examples of the first three:

- Regarding #**1**, someone may say they *believe* in the concept of God as Creator because it's obvious that the Earth, Universe and all living creatures were intelligently designed. Or someone may *believe* homosexuality is intrinsically wrong because the design and function of the sexual organs is obvious (tab 'A' fits into slot 'B'). In both cases the person *believes* **based on what is clearly palpable**.
- Concerning #**2**, people may *believe* they have a brain, even though they've never seen it, because medical science has proven that it exists through dissecting human remains, not to mention brain surgery. So the person *believes* **based on sound data**.
- Regarding #**3**, some may turn to God because the Holy Spirit revealed reality to them and they *believed* it. Their *belief* is based on revelation supplied by the Holy Spirit. Of course any revelation given by the Spirit of truth will correspond to the rightly-divided written Word of truth, which explains Paul's

ministerial guideline for Christian doctrine: "Do not go beyond what is written" (1 Corinthians 4:6).

We observe further insights about faith in that the Scriptures describe it as **the substance of things hoped for** and **being certain of what we do not see** (Hebrews 11:1). The Amplified Bible augments the original Greek text like so:

> Now <u>faith is the assurance (the confirmation, the title deed) of the things [we] hope for</u>, being the proof of things [we] do not see *and* the conviction of their reality [faith perceiving as real fact what is not revealed to the senses].
> **Hebrews 11:1** (Amplified)

Faith is the "**title deed**" of the things we hope for; that is, the things we righteously desire. In short, **faith is the substance that brings the world of hope or desire into reality**! In the Gospels, for instance, people would come to Christ hoping for healing and after receiving it the Lord would say something like "Your faith has healed you" (see, for example, Mark 5:25-34). Faith was the substance that brought them what they hoped for, healing. They were certain — convinced — that the Lord would heal them even though they couldn't yet see it physically.

I trust you're seeing why faith is necessary to receive God's gracious gift of reconciliation and eternal life. After all, how can you receive a gift from someone you don't even believe exists? For example, if you said you had a gift for me and I responded by saying I can't receive it because I don't believe you exist, would you still force the present on me? Of course not. More likely, you'd be irked at my stupidity and arrogance. The same principle applies to those who reject the gospel. When you come across people who do this, be sure to pray that the LORD open their eyes to the truth, i.e. reality.

Did you ever wonder why faith is so important to receiving salvation? Because **faith is nothing more or less than believing God**. That's precisely what Adam & Eve *failed* to do when they were tested in the Garden of Eden and that's why they fell (see Genesis 2:15-3:24). In other words, **the fall of humanity came about due to unbelief and therefore humanity's restoration is dependent upon belief**.

The fall of Adam & Eve in the Garden of Eden, by the way, is actually a showcase of God's grace: The LORD *could* have justly wiped 'em off the face of the Earth for their sin (Romans 6:23), but instead he killed two animals as a substitutionary sacrifice, which provided the temporary covering of sin (Genesis 3:21). This, of course, prefigures the substitutionary death of Christ, which forever cleanses us of the guilt of sin (Hebrews 9:12-15 & 10:4).

I said that there are two keys to receiving God's grace of salvation. Ephesians 2:8-9 (quoted above) only cites one — faith. The reason only faith is cited is because the other key goes hand-in-hand with faith. In short, **they're two sides of the same coin**. This other key is…

<u>4</u>

Repentance

The word 'repent' simply means to change one's mind for the positive, yet this does not refer to a hollow mental exercise. It refers to a real change of mind with **the corresponding actions,** such as the resolve to fulfill God's will (Acts 26:20) and turn from that which is opposed to God's will, i.e. sin (Acts 8:22, 2 Corinthians 12:21 & Revelation 2:21-22). Please look up those passages because they offer a *balanced* understanding of repentance.

We see a broad explanation of what it means to repent here:

> **You were taught, with regard to your former way of life, to <u>put off your old self</u>, which is being corrupted by its deceitful desires; [23] to be <u>made new in the attitude of your minds</u>; [24] and to <u>put on the new self</u>, created to be like God in true righteousness and holiness.**
>
> **Ephesians 4:22-24**

While this passage does not use the word 'repentance,' that's precisely what it's talking about and we see that repentance is a three-pronged practice. It's not just putting off the flesh and the sin it produces, which is how repentance is often defined. This is an *incomplete* definition and therefore a shallow understanding of the subject.

Nor is repentance trying to put on the new self *without* putting off the old self and changing one's thinking. Say you're a parent and have a baby who soils her diaper. How do you resolve the mess? You (1) take the old diaper off, (2) clean her up, and **then** (3) put on the new diaper. Wouldn't it be absurd to put the new diaper over the old diaper? Yet this is what many Christians do in effect when they refuse to put off the old self before putting on the new. They try to put the new man over the old man without changing their thinking and it doesn't work. It's a ticket to utter frustration.

To genuinely repent means to **change one's mind corresponding to a revelation of truth**. This means **changing your thinking** in response to a truth or revelation. If you change your thinking you'll change your actions. The truth or revelation you accept could be based on **1.** obvious reality (that is, truth — the way it really is), **2.** some element of creation, **3.** God's written Word, **4.** spiritual conscience or **5.** the moving of the Holy Spirit (which is arguably synonymous with the previous) or some combination of these.

An Example of Genuine Repentance

Let's consider an example of effective repentance: John Smith is struggling with some form of sexual immorality and he learns from the Scriptures that he needs to "flee from sexual immorality" (1 Corinthians 6:18) so he wisely stops the practice. This is penitence in its most basic form and is the first prong of the three-pronged definition noted above — "putting off the old self." However, if John really wants lasting freedom he's going to have to change his thinking and learn how to walk in the spirit, which are the second and third prongs of repentance.

If he learns to "walk in the spirit" he'll be spirit-controlled rather than flesh-ruled. This is the answer to struggling with any sin because walking in the spirit is one-and-the-same as "putting on the new self" and the new self is "created to be **like God in true righteousness**" (Ephesians 4:22-24, quoted above). This is "walking in the spirit" (Galatians 5:16) wherein you "participate in the divine nature" (2 Peter 1:4) by "clothing yourself in Christ" (Romans 13:14).

Relapses happen, of course, but that's where "keeping with repentance" comes into play (Matthew & Luke 3:8). You don't drown by falling in the water; you drown by staying in the water. If you fall, get back up. Total freedom from the sin is on the horizon. One day you'll look back at it and laugh!

At the very least John is going to have to change his thinking about the immoral practice in question. The reason he kept falling into it was because he *thought* it would be good for him, which was a lie. If he changes his perspective — his mindset — according to the revelation that committing sexual immorality is destructive to his life and his relationship with God, he'll be less prone to committing the sin.

But there are greater truths in which John can base his change in thinking. For instance, God's Word reveals **who the believer is *in* Christ**; for example, the believer is described as:

- dead to sin (Romans 6:11,14,18)
- a child of God (John 1:12-13)
- *reborn* righteous, spiritually speaking (2 Corinthians 5:21)

These are *positional* truths as opposed to *practical* truths; they reveal the believer's **position *in* Christ**. To practice them you simply change your thinking accordingly, which is the second prong of repentance. For instance, John would practice these three positional truths by saying/thinking: "I, John, am dead to sin; I'm a child of God and reborn righteous in my spirit." Since people act according to what they believe, if John thinks & believes he's a child of God, born righteous and is dead to sin he'll naturally begin to act accordingly. This principle is taught in non-Christian circles where it is somewhat effective, how much more so if the individual is spiritually regenerated and indwelt by the Holy Spirit?

So genuine repentance isn't just putting off a sinful practice, it's also changing your thinking and "putting on the new self… created to be like God in true righteousness" (Ephesians 4:22-24).

Repentance *and* Faith

Repentance and **faith** are two sides of the same coin. They go hand-in-hand. This can be observed in these passages:

> **I have declared to both Jews and Greeks that they must <u>turn to God</u> <u>in repentance</u> and <u>have faith</u> in our Lord Jesus.**
>
> **Acts 20:21**

> **"The kingdom of God has come near. <u>Repent</u> and <u>believe</u> the good news!"**
>
> **Mark 1:15**

For repentance to be effective **it must be combined with faith —** which comes through exposure to the LORD and His revelation; this includes God's Word and genuine revelation of the Spirit. If repentance is not combined with faith — belief rooted in God's revelation of reality — it's just a dead exercise and will ultimately fail because true repentance is a genuine "change of mind" with the corresponding actions, as detailed above. This explains, by the way, why **repentance** *and* **faith** are the first two doctrines of the six basic doctrines of Christianity (Hebrews 6:1-2). It's vital to your spiritual health to grasp how repentance and faith work together.

Speaking of the six basic doctrines, they're referred to as **"elementary" Christian teachings** in Hebrews 6:1 and yet there are whole sects and ministries in Christendom that cut *out* one or more of these foundational doctrines or, at least, cut out parts of them. For instance, so-called "radical grace" (or "pure grace") preachers will cut out repentance almost entirely and, if they do teach repentance, they'll emphasize that it's a change of mind while deemphasizing the corresponding actions, which includes "putting off the old self," meaning turning from the "deceitful desires" of the sinful nature (again, Ephesians 4:22-24).

Humility Produces Repentance

Repentance reflects humility because it takes humility to admit you're wrong about something and change your mind. The same goes with feeling remorse and admitting a mistake or transgression. By contrast, an arrogant person is too lofty, selfish, hardhearted and stubborn to change his/her mind with the corresponding actions or feel genuine guilt or confess error. Indeed, pride by its very nature *refuses* to show proper respect toward others, including those in legitimate authority, particularly the Ultimate Authority (God). This again brings to mind this passage:

> **"God opposes the proud
> but gives grace to the humble."**
>
> **James 4:6 & 1 Peter 5:5**

We must get a hold of this: **God literally *opposes* the arrogant**, that is, **he *resists* them**; Proverbs 16:5 even goes so far as to say that "the LORD *detests* all the proud of heart" (emphasis added). Yet, thankfully, God gives his awesome grace to the humble, which means his *favor*. This explains why the LORD only offers the grace of forgiveness to those who are humble enough to acknowledge their transgressions, as shown here:

> **If we claim to be without sin, we deceive ourselves and the truth is not in us. ⁹ If we confess our sins, he is faithful and just and will forgive us our sins and purify us from all unrighteousness.**
>
> **1 John 1:8-9**

"Radical Grace" Preachers Hate 1 John 1:9

Modern-day "radical grace" teachers hate this passage because these preachers stress that all our sins are already forgiven — **including our future sins** — and thus, they say, there's no need to confess them when we miss it. Confessing sin, by the way, is synonymous with repentance because 'fessing up would be useless if not accompanied by a change of mind and the corresponding actions.

One "radical grace" teacher had the audacity to quote 1 John 1:7 to support the idea that all of our future sins are *already* forgiven. Incredibly, he totally ignored the following two verses (verses 8-9, quoted above), which reveal that believers are **obligated to confess**

their sins as they commit them in order to receive forgiveness. This is the **context** of verse 7. Thus the man's error can be traced to ignoring the essential hermeneutical rules — Context is King and Scripture interprets Scripture.

Christ of course died for *all* our sins (Colossians 2:13-14). This includes our *future* sins, and therefore forgiveness is *available* for them, BUT forgiveness of these future sins cannot be **personally appropriated** until AFTER we commit them and humbly confess, as shown above. After all, how can you repent of something you haven't even done (yet)? Moreover, how can God forgive something that hasn't even been committed? This explains the need for 1 John 1:8-9. This dynamic is what John the Baptist was referring to as "keeping with repentance" (Matthew & Luke 3:8). It's in line with what Peter taught concerning born-again believers:

> **But whoever does not have them is nearsighted and blind, forgetting that they have been <u>cleansed from their past sins.</u>**
>
> **2 Peter 1:9**

Believers have been forgiven and cleansed of their "past sins" (other translations say "former sins" or "old sins"). Thus when a person turns to the Lord in repentance and faith *all* their past sins are immediately forgiven, Praise God!

But future sins are a different matter because, again, you can't confess something you haven't even committed. Like I said, forgiveness is readily available for any *future* sins you might commit since Christ bought and paid for *all* our sins through His substitutionary death, but you have to confess future sins after you commit them — repent, change your mind with the corresponding action — in order to be forgiven of them. If you don't do this, these sins won't be forgiven (dismissed) and you'll have to answer for them at the Judgment Seat of Christ, which is the judgment believers must undergo wherein Paul said we'll "receive what is due us for the things done while in the body, whether good **or bad**" (2 Corinthians 5:10-11). The "bad" isn't referring to confessed sins because all confessed sins are already forgiven — dismissed — and you're "purified of all unrighteousness" (1 John 1:9). So the "bad" would include unconfessed sins, whether sins of commission or sins of omission.[2]

Let me share an example of the repentance/forgiveness dynamic from everyday life that we can all relate to: Several years ago I was pulled over on a bypass for changing lanes without using my turn signal. I had just finished a sermon outline for the following Sunday morning and was going to a job; I had a million things going through my mind and didn't have the time or desire to chat with a patrol officer. When he came to my window he noticed an attitude in my words & demeanor and responded, "Now, sir, did I approach you in a disrespectful manner? Why are you giving me an attitude?" In the flash of a second or two I searched my heart and received correction; I made a 180° attitude adjustment and replied, "I'm sorry, sir; I'm on my way to work and have a lot of things on my mind." I then explained that, even though I didn't use my turn signal, I did look before changing lanes and also pointed out that we were the only two vehicles on the highway at the time. Throughout the rest of our conversation I addressed him as "sir" and treated him with sincere respect. This changed the entire course of the incident. Instead of strife and a ticket, our

---

[2] The Greek word for "bad" is *phaulos (FOW-los)* and can refer to moral evil, as well as something worthless, like a bad piece of fruit. Christ clearly used it in the sense of **moral evil** in John 3:20 and John 5:29. *Phaulos* appears only six times in the Greek Scriptures and it's translated as either "bad" or "evil" and not once as "worthless." I share this because "radical grace" preachers try to say that *phaulos* does not refer to moral evil (SMH).

conversation was pleasant and he ended up just giving me a verbal warning.

What saved me from a needless citation? The humility to receive correction, sincerely apologize and show respect. This works in every relationship, including your relationship with the Almighty. Humble repentance is the key that unlocks mercy and forgiveness in all relationships. This simple, powerful principle will bless your socks off if you wisely apply it when appropriate.

Humility is What Makes People "<u>Worthy</u> of the Kingdom of God"

At the risk of sending "radical grace" preachers into cardiac arrest, the New Testament blatantly speaks of those "worthy" of the gift of eternal life. Observe for yourself from the very words of the Mighty Christ and apostle Paul:

> **Jesus replied, "The people of this age marry and are given in marriage. [35] But <u>those who are considered worthy of taking part in the age to come and in the resurrection from the dead</u> will neither marry nor be given in marriage, [36] and they can no longer die; for they are like the angels. They are God's children, since they are children of the resurrection.**
>
> **Luke 20:34-36**

> **Therefore, among God's churches we boast about <u>your perseverance and faith</u> in all the persecutions and trials you are enduring. [5] All this is evidence that God's judgment is right, and as a result you will be counted <u>worthy</u>**

of the kingdom of God, for which you are suffering.

2 Thessalonians 1:4-5

As you can see, Christ spoke of those considered "**worthy of** taking part in the age to come and in the resurrection of the dead" while Paul spoke of those "**worthy of** the kingdom of God." In both cases they were talking about genuine believers worthy of the kingdom of God and the resurrection unto eternal life (1 Corinthians 15:42-44). The Greek word for 'worth' in each passage is *kataxioó (kat-ax-ee-OH-o)*, which simply means "to deem worthy." The Scriptural data we've covered shows that this does *not* refer to being deemed worthy of eternal salvation due to religious works or rituals, but rather being "deemed worthy" due to **genuine humility characterized in repentance and faith** (Acts 20:21).

In conclusion, anyone who wants God's grace of salvation, it's free and you don't have to work for it or purchase it, but **it can only be received through humility; and humility is reflected in the willingness to REPENT and BELIEVE in response to God's revelation, in this case the message of Christ**. This is how you "*obey* the gospel of our Lord Jesus" (2 Thessalonians 1:8) as opposed to *disobeying* the gospel of God (1 Peter 4:17). These are two more verses that send "radical grace" preachers into coronary because they hate the word 'obey' in conjunction with God's grace of salvation. But obeying the message of Christ does not mean working for salvation or trying to buy it; however, it *does* mean responding with humility to God's gracious offer of salvation — which is manifested in repentance and faith. Why? Because **it's humility that attracts God's grace** as opposed to arrogance which naturally repels His favor (James 4:6, 1 Peter 5:5 & Proverbs 3:34). Amen.

The New Testament Started with John the Baptist and his "Baptism of Repentance"

The New Testament started with John the Baptist, as plainly stated by Christ:

> **"The Law and the Prophets** [i.e. the Old Covenant] **were proclaimed <u>until</u> John. <u>Since that time, the good news of the kingdom of God is being preached</u>"**
>
> **Luke 16:16**

The Old Testament ended with John the Baptist who prepared the way for the Messiah via a baptism of repentance (Luke 3:2-4). **With the ministries of John and Jesus the kingdom of God was preached**, not the Law and the Prophets. From John forward "the good news of the kingdom of God has been preached." The "Good News," of course, refers to the awesome message of Christ — the gospel.

So the four Gospels — Matthew, Mark, Luke and John — are *not* Old Testament, but rather the "prologue" to the New Testament and therefore PART OF the New Testament, even though the Church didn't technically start until the Day of Pentecost (see Acts 2:1-13 & 11:15-16). This explains why Christ spoke AS IF the Church was already in function in this passage where he addressed dealing with offending believers:

> **"If they** [the offending believers] **still refuse to listen, <u>tell it to the church</u>; and if they refuse to listen <u>even to the church</u>, treat them as you would a pagan or a tax collector."**
>
> **Matthew 18:17**

As you can see, Jesus spoke *as if* the Church was already in existence even though he had yet to die for our sins and be raised to life for our justification. You could say that the Church was already alive but not birthed yet, like a baby in a mother's womb.

With the understanding that John the Baptist and Jesus Christ preached "the good news of the kingdom of God," notice what the first word of each of their initial sermons was:

> **In those days John the Baptist came, preaching in the wilderness of Judea and saying, "Repent, for the kingdom of heaven is near."**
>
> **Matthew 3:1-2**

> **From that time on Jesus began to preach, "Repent, for the kingdom of heaven is near."**
>
> **Matthew 4:17**

Why did they preach repentance? Because the kingdom of Heaven was near. Similarly, the disciples proclaimed that "the kingdom of God is near" (Luke 10:8-9). Other translations say "the kingdom of God is at hand." The words "near" and "at hand" are translated from the Greek *eggizó (eng-ID-zoh)*, which means "extreme closeness, immediate imminence — even a presence." Whether extremely close or even present to a degree, they preached the kingdom of God and not the Law and the Prophets, which agrees with the Lord's plain declaration in Luke 16:16 above.

Keeping with the full definition of repentance (as detailed above), by saying "repent for the kingdom of God is near" John and Christ were essentially saying "**change your minds, turn from sin** and **turn to the LORD** for the kingdom of God is immediately imminent!" John's "baptism of repentance" was given to "prepare the way for the Lord" (Luke 3:3-4). In other words, John wasn't encouraging people to change their minds & turn from sin and that's it; he was preparing them for the soon-to-come ministry of Jesus Christ, the Word of God, who had "the words of eternal life" (John 6:68). Notice that Jesus didn't have the words of the Law, but rather the words of eternal life. This verse puts it well:

For the law was given through Moses; grace and truth came through Jesus Christ.

John 1:17

When Christ *did* teach on the Law, he focused on the moral Law[3] and the fact that believers achieve the moral Law simply by fulfilling the first and second greatest commands by the Spirit (Matthew 22:36-40). All of this shows that **repentance & faith go hand-and-hand**. They're two sides of the same coin. Genuine repentance — that is, changing one's mind *plus* the corresponding action — is based on faith in God's revelation, whatever that revelation might be.

Why do I point out such obvious things? Because there are "radical grace" preachers who claim that John the Baptist was decidedly Old Testament and therefore he preached the Law in the manner of Old Testament prophets. Many "radical grace" teachers say the same about Christ, but the above proves otherwise.

For details on the Church and when it began, see the article at the Fountain of Life site *When Did the New Testament Start? When Did the Church Begin?*

---

[3] Whilst Christ fulfilled the ceremonial and dietary laws, he didn't teach that believers were obligated to obey them because these laws are done away with in the New Covenant (Colossians 2:16-17, Mark 7:19, etc.). For details see my book *THE LAW and the Believer* or the corresponding article at the FOL site.

5

God's Grace for You Personally

Once obtaining eternal salvation by God's grace (favor), every believer can grow in the LORD's favor on a personal level. We see this in the *example* of Jesus Christ:

> And <u>Jesus grew</u> in wisdom and stature, and <u>in favor</u> *(charis)* with God and man.
>
> **Luke 2:52**

God's grace — favor — was on Jesus (Luke 2:40) and he grew in it. He also grew in favor with people because the fruits of the spirit are attractive and work as **people magnets** (Galatians 5:22-23). This is stressed in the biblical book of wisdom:

> ³ Let <u>love</u> and <u>faithfulness</u> never leave you;
>   bind them around your neck,
>   write them on the tablet of your heart.
> ⁴ Then you will win <u>favor</u> and a good name
>   <u>in the sight of God and man.</u>
>
> **Proverbs 3:3-4**

Both love and faithfulness are fruits of the spirit, which attract the favor — kindness, graciousness — of God and, generally speaking, people too. I say "generally speaking" because the fruits of the spirit will also attract opponents due to their envy, jealousy and rivalry, which incite them against the fruit-bearer. A good example of this is Christ, who walked in the spirit and thus won the hearts of the common Israelites, but he also incurred the ire of the Pharisees and Teachers of the Law.

The prophet Samuel is another good example of growing in favor with God and people (1 Samuel 2:26).

Observe how Peter urged growing in God's favor:

> **But <u>grow in the grace</u> *(charis)* and knowledge <u>of our Lord and Savior Jesus Christ</u>. To him be glory both now and forever! Amen.**
>
> **2 Peter 3:18**

Just as important as it is to grow in the knowledge of the Lord — which is typically stressed in Christendom — it's also vital to **grow in the Lord's grace**; that is, grow in God's *graciousness*, his *favor*. How do you do this? This verse tells us:

> **Come near to God and he will come near to you.**
>
> **James 4:8**

This is a universal law — an *axiom*: **If you come near to the LORD he will come near to you.** And when God comes near to you, you'll naturally have greater favor than if he was distant from you. It's a simple principle verified in the Old Testament (Zechariah 1:3 & Malachi 3:7). It can even be seen in the priestly blessing of the Old Covenant:

> "the Lord make his face shine on you
>   And <u>be gracious to you</u>;
>   the Lord <u>turn his face toward you</u>
>   And give you peace"
>
> **Numbers 6:25-26**

Someone might protest: *"This is favoritism!"* No, favoritism would be denying certain people from growing in God's grace, but that's not the case. *Anyone* — from *any* race, *any* ethnicity, *any* socio-economic class and *any* location — has the opportunity to grow in God's favor. All they have to do is put into practice these simple principles and they'll grow in God's graciousness. Again: **Come near to God and he'll come near to you**.

Two Types of Love and How They Relate to God's Grace

The concept of *having* God's grace and *growing* in it can be observed in the Greek terms translated as "love" in the New Testament, *phileo* love and *agape* love:

1. ***Phileo* love** refers to friendship love or brotherly love, like the platonic affection of David and Jonathan (2 Samuel 1:25-26). Philadelphia, "the city of brotherly love," was named after this type of love. There's an element of affection to *phileo* love; it means there's a bond with the corresponding warmth and respect. The word *phileo (fil-LAY-oh)*, a verb, can be found some 25 times in the original text of the New Testament whereas the noun form, *philia (fil-EE-ah)*, appears only once. Jesus' *phileo* love for Martha, Mary and Lazarus is a good example (John 11:5,35-36).
2. ***Agape* love** refers to ***practical love*** or ***love-in-action*** and is therefore not dependent on affection, respect or closeness. This

can be observed in the Scriptural definition of *agape* love found in 1 Corinthians 13:4-7, which says that *agape (uh-GAHP-ay)* love is patient, kind, does not envy, does not boast, is not proud, is not rude or selfish or easily angered, etc. The word 'love' for God's love for the world in the most popular passage of the Bible is *agape*: "For God so <u>loved</u> the world that he gave his one and only Son, that whoever believes in him shall not perish but have eternal life" (John 3:16). The Creator was walking in love toward all humanity when the Father allowed the Son to die in our place as our substitutionary death; and the Son was willing to die. This was *agape* love, *practical* love, and **not** *phileo* love.

The Bible says that the Father *phileo* loved Jesus when Christ was on Earth (John 5:19-20). Why? Because Jesus diligently sought God (Hebrews 5:7) and imitated the Father, that is, he was godly — *like* God. As such, Jesus grew in God's favor (Luke 2:52). We too can grow in God's favor by coming near to our Creator (James 4:8, 2 Peter 3:18 & Ephesians 5:1).

God loves every person on Earth in a practical sense (John 3:16) — in other words he *agape* loves them — but the LORD does not have *phileo* love for everyone on Earth, that is, affection and respect, a close bond. For instance, God had great *phileo* love for the apostles Paul, Peter and John, but not for arrogant, hateful people like Hitler. Sure, God *agape* loved Hitler — just like God has *agape* loved people all over the Earth throughout history — but he didn't have any affection or respect for Hitler; He wasn't close to Hitler, but he *agape* loved him. Are you following?

Just the same, God is *agape* loving heinous criminals and sick deviants all over the world today — he's walking in *agape* love toward them — but the LORD doesn't have *phileo* love for arrogant abusers, cruel murderers, self-centered rapists, perverse pedophiles and lying gossips & slanderers. The wonderful news for these types of people, and all sinners everywhere, is that when unbelievers respond positively to God's *agape* love — humbly receiving the Lord's grace of salvation through repentance & faith — they automatically attract God's *phileo* love; and this love can grow as their relationship develops.

Think about it in terms of a "teacher's pet," as noted in chapter **1**. I mean "teacher's pet" in a positive sense, not negative. The pupil is the teacher's pet because she's humble; she honors the teacher and is compliant. She does her homework and strives to do well on tests. If she offends the teacher she readily apologizes. The teacher will naturally have *phileo* love for such a student — affection and respect — but he *won't* have affection and respect for a student who is aloof and shows contempt. Of course the teacher will care about the latter student because he's a noble instructor who unbiasedly cares about *all* his students. He wants each one to learn, mature and be successful in life. But when a student is foolish and disrespectful there's only so much the teacher can do. The teacher will walk in *agape* love toward such students — *practical* love — but he will not have *phileo* love for them. Why? Because they're arrogant fools who regard the teacher with contempt. All the instructor can do is continue walking in *agape* love toward them — including praying for them and walking in tough love when required — in the hope that they'll positively respond at some point and turn from their folly.

Now let's relate this to you and God: YOU can grow in God's *phileo* love just like the teacher's pet! "Come near to God and he will draw near to YOU" (James 4:8). It's **an axiom**, a universal law. Strive for a closer relationship with your Creator. Cultivate a more intimate prayer life, which is simply talking with the LORD. Paul instructed us to "pray without ceasing," which indicates a 24/7 bond of communion (1 Thessalonians 5:17). Love God by obeying His instructions, both the general instructions from the written Word and the specific instructions of the living Word, the Spirit of Christ (1 John 5:3). As you do this, you'll grow in God's favor just as surely as Jesus Christ did when he was on Earth (Luke 2:52) and others as well, like Samuel (1 Samuel 2:26).

This is why Peter exhorted believers — you & me — to "**grow in the grace** and knowledge **of our Lord and Savior Jesus Christ**." *DO IT*. This is adding godliness to your faith, as Peter instructed (2 Peter 1:5-9).[4]

Just as God offers grace to his human enemies by walking in practical (*agape*) love toward them, which has the potential to morph into *phileo* love *if* they respond positively to God's grace, so believers are instructed to *agape* love their enemies. This means to walk in *practical* love toward them (Luke 6:35 & Matthew 5:44).

However, we are never commanded to *phileo* love our enemies. Why? Simply because you're not going to have affection & respect for people who hate you without cause and thus disrespect & abuse you. You're *not* going to have a bond of friendship with them. You're *not* going to be close to them. But this doesn't prevent you from walking in *practical (agape) love* toward them — praying for them to come to their senses and receive Christ, returning blessing for cursing, doing good to them even though they don't deserve it. God is only asking us — co-heirs in Christ — to do what he does for his human enemies. Are you following?[5]

---

[4] For details see the article *The Seven Keys to SPIRITUAL GROWTH* at the FOL site or pick up my book *The Four Stages of Spiritual Growth*.

[5] For more details on love in the Bible see the article *The Four Types of Love* at the FOL site.

God's Grace is the Foundation for Living a Godly ("Like-God") Life

Here's another wonderful nugget about God's grace:

> **For the <u>grace</u>** *(charis)* **of God has appeared that offers salvation to all people.** [12] **<u>It teaches us to say "No" to ungodliness and worldly passions,</u> and <u>to live self-controlled, upright and godly lives</u> in this present age,**
>
> **Titus 2:11-12**

It's God's favor that enables believers to say "No" to worldliness and the deceitful desires of the flesh, the sinful nature. It empowers us to live self-controlled, godly ("like-God") lives in this present evil age (Galatians 1:4). How so? It's through God's grace of salvation that we obtain spiritual regeneration (Titus 3:5) and are thus *born* righteous spiritually through the seed of Christ (Galatians 2:21); and, furthermore, are indwelt by the Holy Spirit, our Helper (1 Corinthians 6:19 & John 16:7,13). All this equips us to practice repentance in the genuine three-pronged sense, as covered in chapter <u>4</u> and observed in Ephesians 4:22-24.

Speaking of repentance, it is God's grace — God's kindness — that leads us to repentance:

> **Or do you show contempt for the riches of his kindness, forbearance and patience, not realizing that <u>God's kindness is intended to lead you to repentance</u>?**
>
> **Romans 2:4**

It's the LORD's grace that enables us to be born righteous through spiritual rebirth via the seed of Christ[6]:

> **I do not set aside <u>the grace of God</u>, for if righteousness could be gained through the law, Christ died for nothing!**
>
> **Galatians 2:21**

Needless to say, authentic repentance — that is, (1) changing one's mind based on faith in God's revelation with the corresponding (2) turning from sin and (3) living out of your new nature — does not come about through preaching the Law or simply urging people to *"Turn from sin!"* but rather through declaring God's grace and the truths thereof.

How Do You "Come Near to God"?

So Peter urged us by the Holy Spirit to "grow in **the grace** and **knowledge** of our Lord and Savior Jesus Christ" (2 Peter 3:18). And this is accomplished by drawing near to your Creator which naturally results in the LORD coming near to you (James 4:8). But how do you come near to God? There are two means. One obvious way is by growing in the knowledge of God and putting it into practice or changing your perspective in light of it, making sure of course that what you believe is balanced and "rightly-divided" (2 Timothy 2:15). If you've come this far in this book, you're obviously utilizing this key.

The other key is prayer. Prayer simply means **communion with God** — it's *talking with* your Creator. Jesus' disciples asked him *how* to pray and this was his response:

---

[6] See 2 Corinthians 5:21, Romans 1:17, 1 John 3:9 and 1 Peter 1:23.

"This then is how you should pray:

Our Father in heaven,
hallowed be your name,
your kingdom come,
your will be done on earth as it is in heaven.
Give us today our daily bread.
Forgive us our debts, as we also have forgiven
our debtors.
And lead us not into temptation, but deliver us
from the evil one.
For yours is the kingdom and the power and the
glory forever. Amen"

Matthew 6:9-13

This is typically referred to as "the Lord's prayer" and people sometimes pray it word-for-word, particularly when the occasion calls for a ritualistic or brief prayer to open or close ceremonies. This is fine, but it's really not a prayer to be spoken by rote. "The Lord's prayer" is actually an *outline* of different **types** of prayer. In other words, it's a prayer *skeleton* that needs to be filled in with the "flesh" of our spontaneous prayers according to our unique expressions, communion, needs or desires and the specific people and situations touching us.

The outline can be broken down as such:

- **"Our Father in heaven"** = Communion or fellowship with God.
- **"Hallowed be your name"** = Praise & worship.
- **"Your kingdom come, your will be done on earth as it is in heaven"** = Binding & loosing or intercession, that is, releasing God's will and kingdom into people's lives and situations on Earth, including your own.

- **"Give us today our daily bread"** = Petition, that is, praying for your needs and righteous desires.
- **"Forgive us our debts as we also have forgiven our debtors"** = Repentance, venting, and forgiveness where applicable.
- **"And lead us not into temptation, but deliver us from the evil one"** = Armoring up, protection, watchfulness, speaking in faith, and deliverance.
- **"For yours is the kingdom and the power and the glory forever. Amen"** = Return to praise and close.

As you can see, each part of "the Lord's Prayer" refers to a specific type of prayer.

The First Two Types of Prayer

Let's consider the first two types of prayer from Christ's outline:

"Our Father in heaven" refers to communion with God since the believer is addressing God as his or her "Father." 'Father' indicates *familial* relation and relationship requires communication, hence fellowship. Christianity at its core is a *relationship* with the Creator of the universe, which is why the gospel is referred to as the *message of reconciliation* in 2 Corinthians 5:18-20. Reconciliation means "to turn from enmity to friendship." I encourage all believers to cultivate an intimate relationship with their heavenly Father where you're in constant communion throughout the day, even when you're in bed (Psalm 63:6). Paul referred to this as "praying without ceasing" (1 Thessalonians 5:17 KJV) and the "fellowship of the Holy Spirit" (2 Corinthians 13:14).

Please notice, by the way, that Christ instructed us to pray *to the* Father, not to him (Matthew 6:9). Praying to the Father in the name of Jesus by the power of the Holy Spirit is **prayer protocol** (John 16:23 & verses13-15).

"Hallowed be your name" refers to praise & worship. To 'hallow' means to honor as holy and venerate, that is, treat with respect and reverence. God's name — YaHWeH — represents the Creator Himself so we are to hallow the Great "I Am" (Exodus 3:13-14). The only way you can accomplish this in prayer is by *telling* the Lord. Praise is celebration and includes thanksgiving, raving and boasting, whereas worship is adoration. Praise naturally attracts God's presence and is in accordance with the law of respect: **What you respect moves toward you while what you don't respect moves away from you.** Worship, on the other hand, is adoration or awe, and is the response to being *in* God's presence. See Psalm 95:1-7 and Psalm 100 for verification.

We could further differentiate praise & worship as such:

- Praise celebrates God whereas worship humbly reveres God;
- Praise lifts the LORD up while worship bows when the Lord is lifted;
- Praise dances before the Almighty whereas worship pulls off the Lord's shoes;
- Praise extols the Creator for what He's done while worship adores God for who He is;
- Praise says "Praise the Lord" whereas worship demonstrates that YaHWeH is Lord;
- Praise is thanksgiving for being a co-heir in Christ while worship lays the crown at the LORD's feet.

Every believer is called to deeper praise & worship. It will literally *revolutionize* your life, as it has mine and continues to do so.

Communing with God

It's no accident that **communion with God** and **praise & worship** are the first two kinds of prayer that Christ mentions in his outline (Matthew 6:9-13). They're simply the most important. After all, what does the average father or mother want to hear from their children, particularly as the children grow and develop? Not, "Gimme, gimme," but rather simple communion: "Hi Dad! How are you doing today? You're awesome!" "Do you have time? I'd like to just hang out with you." "Mother, I have something I've been thinking a lot about and I'd like to share it with you to see what you think." "Mom, you're so beautiful!" "Dad, tell me more about that project you're working on in the yard; it's lookin' great so far." Etcetera. If this is the kind of communion our earthly parents prefer why would we think it's any different with our heavenly Father?

You can have these types of conversations with God throughout the day, every day — when you wake up in bed, when you're in the shower, when you're driving, when you're walking down the hall, in the evening, etc. As noted earlier, Paul referred to this as "praying without ceasing" (1 Thessalonians 5:17 KJV) and the "fellowship of the Holy Spirit" (2 Corinthians 13:14). We have to get away from the idea that we only encounter God when we go to church gatherings once or twice a week. This is an Old Testament mentality.

Although the Holy Spirit was active among the Israelites in Old Testament times, it was much different than the way it is with believers in the New Testament. The Holy Spirit's work in that earlier era was limited and selective because the Israelites were spiritually un-regenerated. However, they did have a covenant — a social contract — with God and there were glimmerings of what the Spirit's function would be in the new covenant. David, for instance, was a type of the New Testament believer. Yet there was no spiritual rebirth, no indwelling and no baptism of the Spirit, at least not in the thorough scale we enjoy today.

Simply put, the Israelites were *not* temples of the Holy Spirit as believers are in the new covenant because they weren't spiritually regenerated (Titus 3:5). The temple of God was a literal temple — a building — and before that, a tent tabernacle. Both the Tabernacle of Moses and the Temple of Solomon housed God's presence via the Ark of the Covenant (Exodus 25:22). These structures were literally God's house (although His presence was hidden in the Holy of Holies where the Ark was located, and the High Priest would only enter once a year).

Unless they had an "altar experience,"[7] for the Israelites to encounter God they literally had to go to the Tabernacle or Temple, but — Praise God — this isn't the way it is in the New Testament period because believers are literally the temples of God through spiritual rebirth (1 Corinthians 3:16)!

So attending Christian gatherings at a church facility is not the primary way to connect with God in the New Testament era, although it is *a way* due to the corporate anointing, which Jesus spoke of in Matthew 18:20, not to mention the anointing of fivefold ministry gifts, detailed in Ephesians 4:11-13. Experiencing this "corporate anointing," however, doesn't require going to a specific *building*. It can take place wherever believers meet — a

---

[7] "Altar experiences" involve significant moments for worship (Genesis 8:20), receiving a divine commission (Judges 6:12-24), commemoration (Exodus 17:14–15 & Joshua 22:26–27) and establishing a covenant (Exodus 24:4–8). These somewhat overlap and mark **a notable sequence in one's life involving the LORD** (Genesis 12:7). For details on altar experiences see the article *Altars & Altar Calls and how they're Relevant* at the FOL site.

park, a street corner, the mall, someone's house, a vehicle, the workplace, etc. Even better: Since every believer is the temple of God in the New Covenant period we can encounter the LORD every day. If you're not doing it already, I encourage you to get in the habit of fellowshipping with the LORD on a continual basis, 24/7. It'll revolutionize your walk.

Communing with God in Solitary Places

There's a difference between the 24/7 fellowship noted above and personal prayer sessions. Regarding the latter, Christ said "when you pray, go into your room, close the door and pray to your Father, who is unseen. Then your Father, who sees what is done in secret, will reward you" (Matthew 6:6). Jesus was simply talking about finding a solitary place for a prayer session, known only to you and the LORD. This is in contrast to religious hypocrites who love to pray in front of others, which really isn't communion with God, but rather putting on a show to impress people, which is fakeness, (Matthew 6:5). 'Hypocrite' literally means "actor." This isn't to say, by the way, that it's wrong to pray with other believers, as is shown in the Bible (Acts 12:12), just that it's wrong for believers to pray in front of others for the purpose of impressing them and proving how supposedly godly they are.

When Jesus said to "go into your room, close the door and pray" he was simply talking about finding a solitary place where it's just you and the LORD. It's interesting that Jesus "as was his habit" often went to solitary places in the wilderness to pray, as shown in Mark 1:35, Matthew 14:23 and Luke 22:39-41. How come? Because there's something about nature that's conducive to encountering the Creator.

I think this is why people are attracted to outdoor activities — like hunting, hiking, kayaking, fishing, etc. — because on some primal level they encounter God who is revealed in creation (Psalm 19:1-4, 97:6 & Romans 1:20). Paul & his ministry companions understood this:

> **On the Sabbath we went <u>outside the city gate to the river</u>, where we expected to find a <u>place of prayer</u>.**
>
> **Acts 16:13**

Let me bring something up that all hard-working ministers can relate to: Years ago someone insinuated to me that it must be great to be a full-time minister because of all the supposed time off. I just smiled and allowed him to continue in his arrogant ignorance (although my wife humbly spoke of the constant work and devotion necessary for serving in full-time ministry). The guy simply wasn't aware of what it takes to run a world outreach service, including the determination and focus it takes to regularly write detail-oriented books and articles.

Later that night the Holy Spirit ministered to me and said that the man was ignorant of what it took to even start a world-reaching ministry let alone run one. Images flashed through my mind of literal *years* going out to pray in wilderness areas North, South, East and West of my home, seeking the LORD and interceding, etc. This was well before I even intended to start a ministry. Often I would drive an hour to get to a good spot, sometimes 90 minutes or more. Images of these prayer locations and the sweet communion I had with the Lord flashed through my mind. Of course, this man was completely unaware of all this because I never informed him. Jesus said to keep your prayer sessions to yourself and God. I'm only sharing it here as **1.** An *example* to believers (1 Peter 5:1-4) and **2.** to illustrate that those who seek the

LORD will find Him (Jeremiah 29:13). As you make the LORD first priority — not your *only* priority, but the *first* priority (Matthew 6:33) — the Lord will "direct your paths" (Proverbs 3:5-6).

For an easy-to-understand scriptural way to discern God's will and fulfill it in any stage or level of spiritual growth see the article *How to Obtain Your Desires* at the FOL site (or Chapter Six of my book *The Four Stages of Spiritual Growth*).

Friendship with God

The bottom line is that the LORD wants to be **your friend**, as observed in Exodus 33:11 and John 15:15. Chew on that.

Godliness and Religion — What's the Diff?

I'd like to end this chapter by differentiating godliness and religion, as this ties into walking in God's favor in your everyday life. The Greek word for "godliness" in the Bible is not the same as the Greek word for "religion." The former is *eusebeia (yoo-SEB-ee-ah)* whereas the latter is *thréskeia (thrays-KIH-ah)*. Notice how Greek scholar E.W. Bullinger distinguishes the two:

> *Eusebeia* [godliness] relates to a real, true, vital, and spiritual relation with God while *thréskeia* [religion] relates to the outward acts of religious observances or ceremonies, which can be done in the flesh. Our English word "religion" was never used in the sense of true godliness. It always meant the outward forms of worship. (335)

So **godliness refers to genuine spiritual relationship with the LORD** as opposed to religion, which refers to **outward religious acts**. Godliness *cannot* be performed by the flesh whereas religion can.

Godliness could simply be translated as "like-God-ness." In other words, it's behaving and speaking as the Lord would behave and speak. You could say it's *imitating* God, which we are plainly instructed to do in the Bible

> **<u>Be</u> <u>imitators of God</u>, therefore, as beloved children,**
>
> **Ephesians 5:1**

> **If anyone speaks, <u>they should do so as one who speaks the very words of God</u>. If anyone serves, <u>they should do so with the strength God provides</u>, so that in all things God may be praised through Jesus Christ.**
>
> **1 Peter 4:11**

There are two ways we can imitate God. One is to find out what the Word of God instructs and just put it into practice. The other is simply the result of loving the LORD in a relational sense. How would this make a person godly; that is, *like*-God? Simple: The more time you spend with a person, particularly someone you love and respect, the closer you'll become and the more *like* him or her you'll naturally be. It's the same thing with your relationship with God. The more time you spend with your Creator, the closer you'll become and the more *like* God you'll be. The LORD will "rub off" on you and you'll thus be increasingly *like*-God or godly.

With the understanding of what godliness is, we are encouraged to *pursue* it in the Bible:

> **For the love of money is a root of all kinds of evil. Some people, eager for money, have wandered from the faith and pierced themselves with many griefs.**
> ¹¹ **But flee from these things, you man of God, and pursue righteousness, godliness, faith, love, perseverance and gentleness**
>
> 1 Timothy 6:10-11

We are also encouraged to *train* ourselves to be godly:

> **Have nothing to do with godless myths and old wives' tales; rather, <u>train yourself to be godly</u>. ⁸For physical training is of some value, but <u>godliness</u> has value for all things, holding promise for both the present life and the life to come.**
>
> 1 Timothy 4:7-8

NOTE: Both "godly" in verse 7 and "godliness" in verse 8 are the same Greek word, the aforementioned *eusebeia*.

I'm citing these two passages to stress that godliness — which is an active and increasingly intimate relationship with the LORD (or the natural *result of* such a relationship) — won't automatically happen; it must be pursued and you have to "train yourself" to habitually walk in it. This is understandable when you consider that **all good relationships take time, energy, attention and discipline**. It's no different with your relationship with God.

Godliness Vs. Religion

So godliness and religion are altogether different. Godliness refers to an active relationship with God and the corresponding "rubbing off" effect where you become increasingly like-God whereas religion relates to outward acts of service and devotion. Religion in this sense is good as long as the person balances it out with godliness. However, religion without godliness devolves into sterile go-through-the-motions religiosity.

Godliness involves both simple communion with the Lord and praise & worship. This is understandable when you grasp that praise (celebration) & worship (adoration) are forms of communion. With this in mind, I have to be careful how I word the following because I don't want to be taken the wrong way, so please read with discernment:

Of course it's better to enter into praise & worship once or twice a week in the assembly of the saints than not at all, that's a given. But celebration and adoration of God should become more of an everyday thing as the believer grows. Praise & worship should flow out of us as naturally as water from a spring (Hebrews 13:15). This is the way it should be for growing believers and more seasoned ones alike. But something's seriously wrong if praising & worshipping God becomes mere outward antics at church services. When this happens, the believer is essentially just putting on an act because he or she is around other believers, but it's not a reality in his/her personal life. Beware of falling into this mode because it's a form of legalism — counterfeit "Christianity" — which Christ denounced when he quoted Isaiah:

> **"These people honor me with their lips, but their hearts are far from me."**   **Mark 7:6**

It's possible to praise & worship God with our mouths and yet not really mean it with our hearts. Please be careful to never slip into such a legalistic mode!

Believe it or not, churches sometimes unknowingly facilitate this problem. They put so much stress on coming to every church service and being involved in the assembly that believers end up running around like headless chickens doing this or that for the ministry, which leaves very little time for the most important thing, their *relationship* with God. This is especially so when you factor in other life essentials like work, kids, education, shopping, cooking, physical fitness, rest and recreation.[8] In other words, believers are so pressured to run around doing this or that so their pastors will deem them faithful and godly that they don't have time and energy for the very things that create true godliness — personal time spent with the LORD and God's Word.

This could just as easily happen to pastors and worship leaders or musicians, as well as deacons (workers in the assembly), not to mention traveling ministers. Such people become so involved in the *work* of the ministry that they forsake the core of all Christian service, the Lord himself. The story of Mary and Martha applies here:

> **As Jesus and the disciples were on their way, he came to a village where a woman named Martha opened her home to him. [39] She had a sister called <u>Mary, who sat at the Lord's feet listening to what he said</u>. [40] But <u>Martha was distracted by all the preparations</u> that had to be made. She came to him and asked, "Lord, don't you care**

---

[8] Yes, some measure of recreation is essential: "There's a time to weep and a time to **laugh**, a time to mourn and a time to **dance**" (Ecclesiastes 3:4).

that my sister has left me to do <u>the work</u> by myself? <u>Tell her to help me!</u>"
[41] "Martha, Martha," the Lord answered, "you are worried and upset about many things, [42] but <u>only one thing is needed</u>, Mary has chosen <u>what is better</u> and it will not be taken away from her."

Luke 10:38-42

Martha was so focused on the busy-ness of *working* for the Lord that she unintentionally forsook what was most important — spending time with him and "listening to what he said," which is an obvious reference to spending quality time with the LORD, personally and His Word. In fact, Martha was so involved with the work of her service — her *ministry* — that she got mad at someone else who was free of such concerns and spending personal time with the Lord. So mad, in fact, that she started demanding things from the very One she was supposed to be serving! She *TOLD* the Lord, "Tell her to help me!" This is what religion without godliness does to people: It corrupts them to the point that they end up having the very *opposite* attitude they should have.

Serving God is a wonderful thing, but don't be foolish like Martha and get your priorities out of whack. Think about it, the Living Lord was AT HER HOUSE — the amazing miracle-worker — and all she does is run around in a whirlwind of activity? Mary chose what was more important on this occasion and Jesus even commends her for it. There's a time for doing works of service for the Lord, of course, but there's also a time for your relationship. The latter's more important because **our service for the Lord must spring *from* our love for God**. Otherwise it's just religious works or, worse, putting on a show.

In his aforementioned quote, E.W. Bullinger noted that godliness in the sense of communion with the Lord and worship cannot be performed by the flesh, whereas religious acts can. The flesh gets uncomfortable during praise & worship or intimate prayer. Why? Because it can't handle godliness. But it's perfectly fine performing religious works, including going to church, taking notes, giving an offering or alms, etc. Not that there's anything wrong with those activities, as long as they're balanced out by godliness. The flesh is comfortable working for the Lord or doing things in the name of being devotional rather than spending relational time with the Creator, which was the case with Martha.

<u>6</u>

Responding to a "Radical Grace" Parable

In this chapter and the next one we're going to look at the arguments of "radical grace" ministers to see if their positions mesh with a balanced understanding of the Scriptures. Radical grace is fine as long as it's biblical, but it's not healthy when it's unbalanced and therefore unscriptural.

Let's start with this parable on repentance offered by a "radical grace" preacher:

> 'Let me give you a picture to illustrate true repentance. Suppose a man calls a woman up and gives an invitation to come to his house. She's never been there before and so needs directions. There are two ways the man could direct her: He could give her his address and provide an accurate picture of where he lives. Or he could say, "flee from your house — just drive from your house as fast as possible and don't look back." Do you see the difference? In both cases the woman's going to leave her house. That's guaranteed.
> But only by trusting his directions will she arrive at his house. Repentance is just like that. It's not fleeing from sin like a

Pharisee. It's turning to God in faith. In both cases you will leave your sin. But only by trusting God will you actually arrive someplace better than where you started.'

On the surface this illustration sounds accurate and there are certainly truths contained in it, but the man's perspective on repentance is unbalanced, as verified by a few statements:

'Repentance is just like that. It's not fleeing from sin like a Pharisee. It's turning to God in faith.'

Actually Pharisees *didn't* flee from sin, generally speaking, although they of course gave the outward appearance of doing so, which is a form of legalism. Why else do you think Christ blatantly called them "hypocrites," which literally means "actors"? In other words, he was calling them *fakes*. He also called them "sons of hell," "blind guides," "blind fools," "whitewashed tombs," "full of hypocrisy and wickedness," "snakes" and "brood of vipers"? See Matthew 23:13-33 for verification.

More importantly, repentance is neither one nor the other; it's **both**. The erroneous idea that it's *only* turning to God in faith can be observed in another statement the preacher made:

'Which of the following is the best definition of repentance: (1) to turn from sin or (2) to change your mind?'

By slyly using the "which is the *best* definition" tactic, this minister was trying to get the reader to choose one or the other definition which, by default, rejects the other. I understand where he's coming from because there are shallow ministers who preach repentance as "You must turn from your sin!" and pretty much leave it at that. These types fail to give people New Testament revelation, which would inspire faith and enable them to **change their mind** with the corresponding **putting off of the flesh** and **living out of their new nature with the help of the Holy Spirit**. *That's* true repentance, not merely turning from sin.

The problem with defining repentance as changing one's mind while *disregarding* putting off the old self — the proverbial "turn from sin" — opens the door to the mentality that believers can walk in faith, but they don't necessarily have to put off the old self, that is, turn from sin. This unbalanced mentality explains how the Corinthian church had a man in their midst who was living in fornication with his father's wife and was unwilling to repent; i.e. change his mind and put off the old self. The "old self" in this case was sexual immorality. Thus Paul instructed the assembly to expel the man from the fellowship (1 Corinthians 5:1-5,12-13). Thankfully, the guy later repented and so Paul encouraged the believers to forgive him and warmly welcome him back into their assembly (2 Corinthians 2:6-11). I should point out that Paul was following the instructions that Christ Himself gave on handling an unrepentant believer (Matthew 18:15-17).

This "radical grace" preacher happened to bring up this particular occasion at the Corinth church and wondered why Paul didn't expel numerous others from the fellowship since they were guilty of sins like jealousy, strife and divisive sectarianism (1 Corinthians 3:3-4). Here's why: Paul's very letter — the epistle of 1 Corinthians — was his *initial confrontation* concerning these types of offenses in the Corinth assembly and it remained to be seen if those guilty would repent, i.e. change their minds with the corresponding actions. The fornicator, by contrast, was obviously already confronted a few times and — since he stubbornly refused to change — Paul adamantly instructed the Corinthian elders to expel him, at least until he (hopefully) repented, which the man later did and was therefore welcomed back.

My point is that it was this unbalanced mentality that repentance is merely "changing one's mind" *without* the corresponding turning from the flesh that enabled this man to continue practicing fornication with no qualms in the fellowship at Corinth.

It was this same unbalanced mentality that enabled a woman in the church of Thyatira in Asia Minor (modern-day Turkey) to mislead believers into sexual immorality, which compelled the Lord Christ to rebuke the believers as follows:

> **Nevertheless, I have this against you: You tolerate that woman Jezebel, who calls herself a prophet. By her teaching she misleads my servants into sexual immorality and the eating of food sacrificed to idols. [21] I have given her time to repent of her immorality, but she is unwilling. [22] So I will cast her on a bed of suffering, and I will make those who commit adultery with her suffer intensely, unless they repent of her ways. [23] I will strike her children dead. Then all the churches will know that I am he who searches hearts and minds, and I will repay each of you according to your deeds.**
>
> **Revelation 2:20-23**

"Jezebel" is likely a symbolic name for this supposed prophetess who was misleading believers at the Thyatira fellowship into sexual immorality and other sins. The Mighty Christ points out that he had graciously "given her time to repent **of her immorality**" but she was unwilling to do so. This offers a fuller understanding of repentance as Jesus gave her time to repent — that is, change her mind — but notice it wasn't a pointless changing of the mind as she was to "repent **of her immorality**," that is, change her mind about her immoral ways, which meant putting off the immorality. In other words, turning from it — stopping it.

The same can be observed in Christ's statements about those who committed adultery with this libertine "prophetess" and followed her immoral example: He said he would make them "suffer intensely, unless they repent **of her ways**" (verse 22). You see? Repentance isn't merely the changing of one's mind; it includes putting off the flesh and putting on the new self (Ephesians 4:22-24).

The Lord goes on to say that he would "strike her children **dead**," obviously referring to Jezebel's *spiritual* children who followed her example and stubbornly refused to repent. This is the divine judgment of premature death. Many modern Westernized believers find such a thought incredulous due to the unbalanced diet their pastors feed them, but in the Scriptures we observe this same thing happened in the Corinth church where unrepentant believers brought judgment upon themselves and thus some of them were wiped off the face of the Earth (1 Corinthians 11:27-32). This doesn't mean they lost their eternal salvation, but they did incur the judgment of premature death, as did Ananias and Sapphira (Acts 5:1-11). The positive side to accounts like this is that they inspire the fear of the Lord (see verse 11), which promotes holiness — changing one's mind in light of the revelation of God; this motivates putting off the flesh and putting on "the new self, which is **created to be like God in true righteousness and holiness**" (again Ephesians 4:22-24).

Christ also exhorted believers from other assemblies to repent of one negative thing or another; for instance, the church in

Pergamum (Revelation 2:15-16) and the believers in Laodicea (Revelation 3:19).

Plain passages like these cause "radical grace" preachers to hyperventilate. They thus totally ignore them and hope that no one brings them up. But we have to be balanced with God's word. When we draw conclusions on a topic, like grace, we cannot discard relevant "pieces of the puzzle"; rather, we must make sure that all the Scriptural "pieces" fit together. Our conclusions should be as "watertight" as possible. That's what this book is all about — putting all the pieces of the scriptural puzzle on grace together without unsoundly discarding relevant passages.[9]

Now let's return to the "radical grace" parable:

'Suppose a man calls a woman up and gives an invitation to come to his house. She's never been there before so needs directions. There are two ways the man could direct her: He could give her his address and provide an accurate picture of where he lives. Or he could say, "flee from your house — just drive from your house as fast as possible and don't look back." Do you see the difference? <u>In both cases the woman's going to leave her house. That's guaranteed.</u>'

Actually, it's *not* guaranteed that the woman's going to leave her house. What if she simply refuses the invitation? What if she's not very smart and — even though the man provided directions to his house — she stubbornly refuses to leave *her* abode? Or what if she's a homebody who prefers to stay home and "visit" the man's house via Skype, phone or email? In such cases, it would be

---

[9] See the article *Hermeneutics — Proper Bible Interpretation* at the FOL site.

necessary for the man to not only provide his address, but **also encourage the woman to leave her house**.

'But only by trusting the man's directions will the invited woman arrive at his house.'

No, only by **1.** trusting the man's directions *and* **2.** willingly leaving her house will she arrive.

'Only by trusting God will you actually arrive someplace better than where you started.'

Only by trusting God enough to *obey* the details of the Lord's instructions, which includes leaving where you are; otherwise one's trust — faith — is questionable.

Okay, that's enough of this faulty parable. Let's consider some other "radical grace" arguments...

Responding to other "Radical Grace" Arguments

Here are further "radical grace" arguments that we need to examine in light of the rightly-divided Scriptures:

'If grace is the only thing that teaches us to say no to ungodliness, guess what you should preach. Grace!'

True — as shown in Titus 2:11-12 — but what is it that unlocks God's grace in a person's life? **Humility** (James 4:6 & 1 Peter 5:5). After all, God *opposes* the proud. Furthermore, humility is the root of both repentance and faith, which open the door to eternal salvation (Acts 20:21 & Mark 1:15).

Responding to the message of Christ with genuine humility and the corresponding repentance & faith is what it means to "**obey** the gospel of our Lord Jesus" (2 Thessalonians 1:8). It's those who are arrogant who "**do not obey** the gospel of God," which means they refuse to humbly repent and believe (1 Peter 4:17).

"Radical grace" preachers loathe these verses because they hate the word "obey" used in connection with salvation. They hate the idea that people have a *responsibility* to humbly receive the message of Christ. Yet the gift of salvation is not forced upon anyone.

> **'It's all about Jesus and what He has done. It's not about me and what I do. See Him, know Him, fix your eyes on Him, marvel at Him and repentance will follow naturally.'**

While I understand where this argument is coming from and there's certainly some good truth in it, God's grace of salvation *is* dependent upon what the person does or doesn't do, as plainly shown above. The individual *is* responsible for "obeying the gospel of our Lord Jesus." This doesn't mean the gift of salvation is worked for or purchased, but it does have to be received by those "worthy" candidates (Luke 20:34-36 & 2 Thessalonians 1:4-5) who respond to God's grace with **humility** characterized in the willingness to **repent** and continue in **faith**.

> **'Repentance literally means "change your mind" — nothing more, nothing less.'**

Wrong, it means changing one's mind **with the corresponding action**, like the resolve to fulfill God's will (Acts 26:20) and turn from that which is opposed to God's will, i.e. sin (Acts 8:22, 2 Corinthians 12:21 & Revelation 2:20-23). Why do you think Christ urged the transgressing Thyatirans to "repent of [their] immorality"? (Revelation 2:21-22).

'Paul said we must rightly-divide the Word — that is, emphasize certain scriptures over others. It follows that it must be possible to wrongly-divide the Word — emphasize the wrong scriptures over others.'

But "rightly dividing the Word" (or "properly handling" it, as the NIV puts it) **does *not* mean to discard relevant passages**. As noted earlier, *all* the applicable pieces of the Scriptural puzzle must fit and one's conclusions must be watertight or, at least, as watertight as possible. This is what this book does with the topic of grace whereas "radical grace" preachers regularly cut out pertinent passages to support their unbalanced take on the subject. For instance, you'll rarely, if ever, hear them mention 2 Peter 3:18, Luke 20:34-36 and 2 Thessalonians 1:4-5 or Acts 8:22, 2 Corinthians 12:21 and Revelation 2:21-22. Passages like these send them into uncontrollable spasms of spiritual arrest.

'In Luke 24:47 Jesus says the forgiveness or remission of sins will be proclaimed in His name to all nations'

Let's read the passage to see what Christ specifically said:

> **"This is what is written: The Messiah will suffer and rise from the dead on the third day, [47] <u>and repentance for the forgiveness of sins</u> will be preached in his name to all nations, beginning at Jerusalem."**
>
> **Luke 24:46-47**

While Jesus died for everyone's sins throughout history and therefore bought forgiveness for us (Colossians 2:13 & 1 Peter 3:18) notice that *repentance* **is a condition for people to personally appropriate that forgiveness**. This explains why

Christ and the apostles preached repentance & faith (Mark 1:15 & Acts 20:21) and why **repentance & faith are the first two doctrines of the six basic doctrines of Christianity**, which are "elementary" teachings (Hebrews 6:1-2), meaning they're fundamental to Christianity and therefore those ministers who fail to teach them are askew and out-of-balance.

'Have our sins been forgiven or haven't they? Paul thought so (Colossians 2:13). Peter thought so (2 Peter 1:9). John thought so (1 John 1:7 & 2:12). I think so.'

When a person humbly turns to the Lord in repentance & faith in response to the gospel all their *past* transgressions are forgiven, which explains Peter emphasizing "past sins" in 2 Peter 1:9, a verse this minister cites. Future sins, however, are a different story because — although Christ paid the penalty for them — a person cannot receive forgiveness for them until **1.** they commit the sin in question and **2.** confess to the LORD. After all, how can a person confess and receive forgiveness for something they haven't even done yet? This is why 1 John 1:9 is sandwiched between the verses this man cites. Speaking of which, why did he omit such a relevant passage on the topic contained in the very context of the verses he cites as proof texts? I'll tell you why, it contradicts his unbalanced idea that all future sins are *already* forgiven and so there's no need to confess them and appropriate forgiveness.

'The point is not that the tax-collector "beat his breast" but that he <u>asked</u>. This is the sole condition for receiving grace and mercy — you have to ask for it. You can ask with weeping, like this man, or boldly, like the Canaanite woman (Matthew 15:21-28) — as long as you admit your need for grace you'll get it.'

This supports the fact that **humility opens the door to God's grace**, as has been stressed throughout this book. Let's read the passage in question about the tax-collector who "beat his breast":

> **To some who were confident of their own righteousness and looked down on everyone else, Jesus told this parable:** [10] **"Two men went up to the temple to pray, one a Pharisee and the other a tax collector.** [11] **The Pharisee stood by himself and prayed: 'God, I thank you that I am not like other people — robbers, evildoers, adulterers — or even like this tax collector.** [12] **I fast twice a week and give a tenth of all I get.'**
>
> [13] **"But the tax collector stood at a distance. He would not even look up to heaven, but beat his breast and said, 'God, have mercy on me, a sinner.'**
>
> [14] **"I tell you that this man, rather than the other, went home justified before God. For all those who exalt themselves will be humbled, and those who humble themselves will be exalted."**
>
> **Luke 18:9-14**

The reviled tax collector "went home justified before God" because he humbled himself before the Almighty and asked for mercy. He was obviously willing to repent — change his mind with the corresponding action. The Pharisee, on the other hand, did not go home justified before God. Why? Because he was arrogant and absurdly boasted of all his "great" religious works when he stood before the LORD at the Temple. This parable effectively illustrates the fundamental truth emphasized throughout this book: **"God opposes the proud but gives his grace to the humble."**

'People need to hear how much God loves them.'

Absolutely. They need to hear how far God has bent over backwards, so to speak, to reconcile lost, sinful humanity. This is the radical example of loving one's enemies — suffering horribly and dying for them; in this case, in the hope of reconciling with them and providing eternal life (2 Corinthians 5:18-20). And, yes, apart from redemption lost people *are* enemies of God (Romans 5:10), which isn't to say that every unsaved soul is frothing at the mouth with malevolent evil.

As explained in chapter **5**, the LORD loves his human enemies in the sense of *agape* love, which is *practical* love; thus Christ died for us (John 3:16). The Almighty is hoping this gets their attention, that they "come to their senses" and transfer "from the dominion of Satan to God" (Acts 26:18). But the Almighty doesn't have *phileo* love — affection, respect, closeness — for arrogant fools who spurn the Creator' graciousness. God doesn't have "warm fuzzies" for those who stubbornly and selfishly continue on in their sin, like lying slanderers. The LORD is not up in Heaven affectionately reflecting on sick pedophiles: "Oh, I just luvvy wuvvy these vile abusers of children." NO! God *opposes* them — *resists* them.

We see this in the case of Saul, who was radically persecuting the early Church: The Lord appeared to him and asked why he was persecuting Him (his body, the Church) and proceeded to strike Saul with blindness (Acts 9:1-19). This is an example of *tough* love.[10] Saul was a tough nut to crack, but he wisely responded to the Lord's tough love tactics by humbling himself and praying, to which the Lord sent Ananias, who laid hands on Saul and he was healed. Thus Saul became the apostle Paul, God's mightiest human agent in the New Testament era.

---

[10] See the article *Gentle Love and Tough Love* at the FOL site.

But it could have gone the other way: Saul *could've* arrogantly spurned the Lord & his instructions and suffered the inevitable consequences. A good example of this is King Herod Agrippa I, who reigned over Judea from 41-44 AD. Like Saul, Herod started to severely persecute the Church, even putting James, the brother of John, to the sword and imprisoning Peter (Acts 12:1-5). The Lord mercifully gave Herod much time to repent, but Herod refused and pompously continued on in his sin and thus an angel of the Lord wiped him off the face of the Earth (Acts 12:19-23). Truly, God opposes the proud, but gives grace to the humble!

'They need to hear about his unconditional favor and grace.'

Actually the Greek word for 'favor' or 'grace' — *charis* — simply means "graciousness, favor, kindness." Contrary to what this man heard in seminary it doesn't mean "*unconditional* favor." If God's grace of salvation was truly "unconditional," as this man & others claim, then *everyone* will be saved, whether they humbly turn to God in repentance & faith or not, which is not what the Scriptures teach. That is Universalism, a false doctrine easily negated by numerous plain passages.[11]

It is true that God's grace of salvation is unmerited in the sense that it cannot be bought and you can't work for it. Yet this doesn't mean there aren't conditions to receiving it. Humility is the necessary condition that unlocks God's grace in a person's life (James 4:6, 1 Peter 5:5 & Proverbs 3:34) and humility is the root of both repentance and faith, as explained elsewhere. In other words, the only ones who merit God's grace are those humble souls who are willing to "obey the gospel" through repentance & faith. These

---

[11] For details see the article on Universalism at the FOL site.

are the ones who are "worthy of the kingdom of God" (2 Thessalonians 1:4-5).

'When the Corinthian Christians fell into sin, Paul still didn't preach "turn from sin." Instead he reminded them of their identity in Christ. He understood that grace, not dead works, is the cure for sin.'

Yes, some of the Corinthians fell into jealousy, strife and sectarianism, which is why Paul corrected them in his first letter (1 Corinthians 3:3). By "corrected them" he clearly encouraged them to put off such fleshly works. He even emphasized that they "flee from sexual immorality" "and stop sinning," both of which certainly sound like "turn from sin" to me (1 Corinthians 6:18 & 15:34).

But, in keeping with the proper understanding of repentance, Paul didn't just urge them to flee from sin, he also told them *who they were in Christ* to give them a revelation on which to base their faith. For instance, he stressed that they were a "temple" of God (1 Corinthians 6:19-20) and conveyed several other such truths in his subsequent letter (e.g. 2 Corinthians 5:17,21 & 8:9).

'Regarding 2 Corinthians 7:8-11, Paul is saying, "I don't regret what I did." '

What did Paul do and why didn't he regret what he did? Let's read the passage:

Even if I caused you sorrow by my letter, I do not regret it. Though I did regret it — I see that my letter hurt you, but only for a little while — [9]yet now I am happy, not because you were made sorry, but because your sorrow <u>led you to repentance</u>. For you became sorrowful as God intended and so were not harmed in any way by us. [10] Godly sorrow brings repentance that leads to salvation and leaves no regret, but worldly sorrow brings death. [11] See what this godly sorrow has produced in you: what earnestness, what eagerness to clear yourselves, what indignation, what alarm, what longing, what concern, what readiness to see justice done. At every point you have proved yourselves to be innocent in this matter.

2 Corinthians 7:8-11

Paul caused the Corinthian believers sorrow by his previous letter (the epistle of 1 Corinthians). Why did his epistle cause them sorrow? Because it identified their sins and corrected them; he urged them to repent and even insisted that they expel an unrepentant fornicator. All this was detailed in the previous chapter. Paul didn't regret what he said because it made them sorrowful and **led to their repentance**. This shows, by the way, that the Corinthians repented in response to Paul's confrontation in his first letter; and this is why none of them were expelled. Thankfully, even the man who was expelled repented and hence Paul urged them to warmly allow him back into their fold (2 Corinthians 2:6-8).

You see, it was necessary for Paul to preach *biblical* repentance on this occasion and it bore good fruit at the Corinth assembly. Sometimes it will be necessary for you or me to preach repentance as well, as led of the Spirit, which includes urging people to put off the flesh. "Radical grace" preachers who hate the idea of preaching repentance — at least in the sense of turning from sin — need to get a hold of this.

'I change my way of thinking so that my life lines up with what is true. I repent every day and it's wonderful.'

That's great, Praise God! I encourage this man — and other "radical grace" preachers — to preach *biblical* repentance to their congregants/readers/followers, but repentance in its complete sense, not just useless mental assent. 'Radical grace' teachers in general tend to downplay "putting off the flesh," one way or another.

'The key to life is not in turning from sin but trusting in Jesus.'

I don't understand why this man insists that it's one or the other. It's **both**. If "the wages of sin is death" then it naturally follows that *turning away from* sin must be turning *away* from death (Romans 6:23). It's why Christ admonished: "unless you repent, you too will all perish" (Luke 13:3,5). In other words, repentance (in the sense of turning away from sin) is a step in the right direction, toward life. This is why the biblical book of wisdom says that "correction and instruction are **the way to life**" (Proverbs 6:23). When a person is in error and receives correction or instruction and turns from his/her error, it's **the way to life**.

Of course "trusting in Jesus" is the key to life because Christ is "the way and the truth and the life" (John 14:6) and thus has "the words of eternal life" (John 6:63,68).

Yet having faith in Christ and stubbornly refusing to turn from the deceitful desires of the flesh is not life. It's this kind of libertine folly that *enabled* the unrepentant fornicator at the Corinth assembly and eventually caused him to get expelled (1 Corinthians 5:13); it's what brought about the premature deaths of others in Corinth (1 Corinthians 11:29-32); it's what caused Jezebel's followers in Thyatira to suffer intensely, with the most stubbornly impenitent ones prematurely dying (Revelation 2:20-23)!

So the key to life is **1.** turning from sin and **2.** turning toward the Lord in faith. That's why Paul preached repentance *and* faith, not one or the other (Acts 20:21); it's why repentance and faith are the first two of the six basic doctrines of Christianity (Hebrews 6:1-2). It's why repentance & faith go hand-in-hand.

Needless to say, "radical grace" teachers, like this man, are *really* teaching **unbalanced grace** because they regularly discard relevant passages on the topic. And they'll have to answer for it at the Judgment Seat of Christ (see James 3:1 & 2 Corinthians 5:10-11).

Let's not be foolish like that; let's be thorough in our studies — including on the topic of grace — and "watch our life **and doctrine** closely" (1 Timothy 4:16). Some unwise ministers, unfortunately, are *not* watching their doctrine.

<u>Closing Word</u>

I trust you've been blessed by this study and have a fuller understanding of God's grace for salvation and how to grow in God's favor in your everyday life.

May the LORD bless you in your service as you cultivate humility, draw closer to God, seek the truth and apply what you've learned.

Amen.

Bibliography

Brown, Francis/Driver, S.R./Briggs, Charles A. *Brown-Driver-Briggs Lexicon*. Peabody: Hendrickson Publishers, 1994

Bullinger, Ethelbert W. *A Critical Lexicon and Concordance to the English and Greek New Testament*. Grand Rapids: Zondervan Publishing House, 1975

Helps Word-Studies Lexicon. Retrieved from Biblehub.com. 1987, 2011

LORD, The. *Berean Study Bible (BSB)*. Bible Hub, 2016

LORD, The. *English Standard Version (ESV)*. *Holy Bible*. Chicago: Crossway, 2001

LORD, The. *Good News Translation*. *Holy Bible*. The Bible Society, 2001

LORD, The. *International Standard Version*. *Holy Bible*. Davidson Press, 1999

LORD, The. *King James Version*. *Holy Bible*. Iowa Falls: World Bible Publishers

LORD, The. *New American Standard Bible*. *Holy Bible*. Nashville: Holman, 1977

LORD, The. *New International Version*. *Holy Bible*. Nashville: Holman, 1986

LORD, The. *New International Version (Revised)*. *Holy Bible*. Nashville: Holman, 2011

LORD, The. *New King James Version Study Bible: Second Edition*. Nashville: Thomas Nelson, 2012

LORD, The. *New Living Translation*. Carol Stream: Tyndale House Publishers, 2006

LORD, The. New Revised Standard Version. Holy Bible. Nashville: Nelson, 1989

LORD, The. *The Amplified Bible.* Grand Rapids: Zondervan, 1987

LORD, The. *Quest Study Bible: New International Version.* Grand Rapids: Zondervan, 2003

LORD, The. *World English Bible (WEB).* Salt Lake City: Project Gutenberg, 2013

LORD, The. *Weymouth New Testament.* Ulan Press, 2012

LORD, The. *Young's Literal Translation (YLT).* Grand Rapids: Baker Books, 1989

Strong, James. *Strong's Exhaustive Concordance.* Grand Rapids: Baker, 1991

Vine, W.E. *Vine's Expository Dictionary of Biblical Words.* Cambridge: Nelson, 1985

Fountain of Life

Teaching Ministry

(Psalm 36:9)

The mission of Fountain of Life is to **set the captives FREE** by **reaching the world** with the **life-changing truths of God's Word**, the **power of the Holy Spirit** and the **Awesome News of the message of Jesus Christ**.

We're calling Spiritual Warriors all over the Earth to partner with us on this mission!

Books by Dirk Waren:

The Believer's Guide to FORGIVENESS & WARFARE
Legalism Unmasked
HELL KNOW! (full and condensed versions)
SHEOL KNOW! (full and condensed versions)
The Four Stages of Spiritual Growth
ANGELS: Their Purpose and Your Responsibility
THE LAW and the Believer
The SIX BASIC DOCTRINES of Christianity
GRACE: What is It? How Do You Grow in It?
How to Handle OFFENSES: Personal & Criminal